Little Guides to
Great Lives

FERDINAND MAGELLAN

Published in 2019
by Laurence King Publishing Ltd
361–373 City Road
London EC1V 1LR
United Kingdom
Tel: +44 20 7841 6900
E-mail: enquiries@laurenceking.com
www.laurenceking.com

Illustrations © 2019 Dàlia Adillon

Written by Isabel Thomas

ISBN: 978-1-78627-401-4

Commissioning Editors: Chloë Pursey and Leah Willey
Senior Editor: Charlotte Selby
Design concept: Charlotte Bolton
Design: The Urban Ant Ltd.
Production: Felicity Awdry
Series title designed by Anke Weckmann

Printed in China

Other *Little Guides to Great Lives*:
Marie Curie
Charles Darwin
Amelia Earhart
Anne Frank
Frida Kahlo
Leonardo da Vinci
Nelson Mandela

Little Guides to
Great Lives

FERDINAND
MAGELLAN

Written by
Isabel Thomas

Illustrations by
Dàlia Adillon

Laurence King Publishing

Ferdinand Magellan
1480–1521

Imagine planning the biggest, boldest expedition EVER ... and then being told you can't go! This is what happened to Portuguese explorer Ferdinand Magellan.

But steely Magellan let nothing stand in his way. Against all odds, he headed out to sea and led the first European voyage to circumnavigate the globe. It is remembered as one of the most epic journeys of all time—full of mutiny, storms, starvation, and sharks.

Despite these dangers, Magellan discovered an "impossible" short cut, named an ocean, and proved beyond doubt that our planet is round.

For someone so famous, Magellan's early life is a bit of a mystery. He was born in Portugal in 1480, but no one knows exactly when or where. Magellan grew up in the countryside and his parents were both from rich, noble families.

Rodrigo de Magalhães
(Father)

Alda de Mesquita
(Mother)

6

In Portugal, Ferdinand was known as Fernão. Later, when he grew up and moved to Spain, he became known as Fernando de Magallanes.

Thanks to his parents' high status, Ferdinand had the best education in the country—he joined the royal court in Lisbon, the capital city in Portugal, to work as a <u>page</u>. As well as running errands and waiting on the queen, ten-year-old Ferdinand learned ...

... music

... reading and writing

... horse riding

... dancing

... falconry

... sword-fighting

... and navigation using the sun, moon, and stars!

This was the perfect preparation for the top jobs available in late-fifteenth-century Portugal, which was becoming one of the world's most powerful countries by taking control of the seas.

In 1496, the teenaged Magellan was promoted to the rank of <u>squire</u>. He worked in the king's <u>marine</u> department, stocking ships with everything they needed to set off on long and daring adventures. It was an exciting place to be …

Just three years earlier, Christopher Columbus had sailed into Lisbon on his way back from the first ever European voyage to the Americas. He received a hero's welcome.

And in 1498, Portuguese explorer Vasco da Gama found a sea route to India, by sailing all the way around Africa. His ships returned in 1499, laden with jewels, exotic materials, and spices.

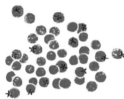

Spices such as pepper, cinnamon,
and cloves were not grown in
Europe, so they could be sold
for thousands of times their
original price, once they had been
brought back across the seas.

Suddenly everyone wanted to seek their fame and fortune at sea, sailing from Lisbon, around Africa, to the <u>Far East</u>. All Magellan could do was help stock their ships, and wait ...

... and at last, his turn finally came.

In 1505, Magellan joined an important expedition to India and the Far East. Portugal was now leading the way in European exploration of the world's oceans. Portuguese sailors had set up bases all along the coasts of Africa, where ships could stop and stock up on food and water.

Controlling these stop-off points meant control of trade and a steady flow of wealth back to Portugal. But the Portuguese weren't the only ones doing this. Egyptian, Arab, and Indian explorers also wanted to control major ports in the Indian Ocean. Dangerous battles happened all the time.

Magellan joined a fleet of 22 ships, sent to seize control of the Indian Ocean for Portugal, at whatever cost!

The expedition lasted almost eight years. Magellan traveled in Africa, India, and parts of Asia, and fought in several battles.

In 1509, Magellan helped the Portuguese to win power over most of the Indian Ocean.

In 1511, the expedition took control of the Strait of Malacca—the bit of sea that all ships traveling east to west had to go through.

Some ships explored the Moluccas, known as the Spice Islands. Magellan learned how rich they were in precious spices.

European exploration and <u>expansion</u> came at a terrible cost. The people already living in the countries being explored were often treated badly. Land was seized using force. Property was stolen. Local people were killed or taken prisoner and sold as <u>slaves</u>. Although Magellan took part in these actions, at the time he became known for being different. He tried to act more fairly and to lead by example.

When he finally returned to Lisbon, Magellan asked the Portuguese king for money to set up his own trading business and did everything he could to impress him. He volunteered for a dangerous mission to Morocco to stop a <u>rebellion</u> and he proposed new and exciting ideas for expeditions. But the king thought Magellan was trouble and refused all of his requests.

Magellan's grandest plan was to find a brand-new route to the Spice Islands! His wild idea was to reach the East by sailing west—something that no sailor had ever done. Once again, the king said "No!"

But Magellan didn't give up. He decided to ask if he could offer his services to Spain instead of Portugal.

Neighboring Spain was also a great naval power. Portugal and Spain were such fierce rivals that, in 1494, they had to agree to divide up the world between them (at that time, they didn't care that it wasn't theirs to divide). They did this by drawing a line on a map.

All newly discovered (and yet to be discovered) territories west of the line were given to Spain ...

The map used to draw up the Treaty of Tordesillas looks very different from today's maps. This is because no European had ever been to the other side of the world and had no clue that there was a huge ocean there. Some people were still convinced that the Earth was flat!

The Treaty of Tordesillas (1494)

N
W E
S

... and all newly discovered (and yet to be discovered) territories east of the line were given to Portugal.

In 1517, Magellan moved to Spain and began work on his new plan: to prove that it's possible to reach the East by sailing in the opposite direction and to persuade the Spanish king to give him the money to do it! For three years, Magellan scoured libraries in Portugal and Spain, reading everything he could find about geography and pouring over every map.

By making friends in the right places, Magellan got the chance to tell the Spanish king about his plan. The king thought the plan sounded amazing. It would mean that Spanish ships could reach the Far East without having to go around Portuguese-controlled Africa. The king offered to pay for the whole expedition.

Give me some money, and I'll find a quicker route to the Spice Islands AND prove that they lie in Spain's half of the world!

I promise to outfit five ships for you, equipped with crew, food, and weapons to last two years.

Magellan set about preparing for the journey, but it didn't go smoothly. Spanish officials were outraged that the expedition would be led by Portuguese captains. Portuguese officials were outraged that Magellan was now working for the Spanish. Both sides tried to wreck the project.

The fleet itself was also not as good as it had sounded. The five ships provided by the king were tiny, old, and rotting.

Magellan worked hard and soon the boats were
fixed up and loaded with supplies for the voyage:

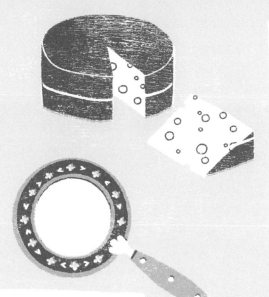

FOOD
beans
chickpeas
lentils
200 barrels of anchovies
dried fish and meat
3 live pigs
7 live cows
984 cheeses
250 strings of garlic
3 jars of capers
(no one likes capers)

GOODS TO TRADE
copper
cloths
silks
bells
mirrors
crystals
colored handkerchiefs
fish hooks
bracelets
knives
scissors

WEAPONS
1,000 lances
200 pikes
120 javelins
1,100 darts
60 crossbows
4,300 arrows
swords
armor
2,540 kilograms
of gunpowder

On 20 September 1519, the five ships finally set off from Spain, firing their cannons in joy. They were heading off into the unknown, on a journey that was not only daring but which might prove impossible. The risk of death was huge. But the rewards were also huge. Magellan would receive a share of any treasures and his family would help to <u>govern</u> any newly discovered lands.

San Antonio
Captain:
Juan de Cartagena
(Spanish)
57 crew

Trinidad
Captain:
Ferdinand Magellan
(Portuguese)
62 crew

Concepción
Captain:
Gaspar de Quesada
(Spanish)
44 crew

More than 230 men were squeezed on board the tiny ships, including Portuguese, Spaniards, Basques, Italians, French, Flemish, Germans, Greeks, Africans, Moors, Madeirans, and an Englishman. Enrique, a man who Magellan had bought as a slave in Malacca on an earlier expedition, was also on board. He would be a translator when they reached their destination.

Victoria

Captain:
Luis de Mendoza
(Spanish)
45 crew

Santiago

Captain:
João Serrão
(Portuguese)
31 crew

Magellan's plan to get to the East by sailing west began with crossing the vast Atlantic Ocean. He would search for a natural passageway or "strait" that would allow ships to pass through the enormous landmass that stood in their way—the Americas.

Magellan had read about an <u>estuary</u> that had been spotted by a Spanish explorer. That crew hadn't managed to explore much of it—some were captured and the rest fled! But Magellan wasn't scared. He thought it sounded like the perfect place to start.

There were no radios in the 1500s, so Magellan ordered the other ships to follow his flag by day and his lantern by night. The Spanish captains were not happy. There were already too many rules to follow. Magellan had banned swearing and gambling. Officers were even expected to be kind to the crew!

What are we supposed to do for fun?

RULES

After getting stuck in the <u>doldrums</u> near the coast of Africa, the fleet had to battle through fierce storms to reach the <u>equator</u>. They finally spotted the coast of Brazil more than two months after setting off. The fleet landed two weeks later, in the area where Rio de Janeiro is today. Magellan had ordered his crew to treat native people in the lands they visited with respect.

One of the crew was a 27-year-old Italian <u>scholar</u> called Antonio Pigafetta.

Antonio Pigafetta

Pigafetta went along on the journey to see "the wonderful things of the ocean." It's thanks to his detailed diary that we know so much about the voyage.

He wrote about the people they met in Brazil and how easy it was to trade metal objects for fresh food and animals.

A bell for a whole basket of potatoes that taste like chestnuts and are as long as turnips.

My best swap was a king of diamonds from a pack of playing cards for six hens.

A pair of scissors for enough fish for ten men.

A mirror for eight parrots.

Stocked up with food and water, the fleet continued to sail down the coast of South America until they reached the estuary that Magellan was looking for. The crew were worried about <u>cannibals</u>, but Magellan insisted they explore the estuary, searching for a way through.

It was not to be ...

The water is fresh, not salty. It can't lead to an ocean!

The estuary was not the entrance to a strait, but the exit of a river—now known as the Rio de la Plata. Magellan explored more channels as the fleet traveled down the coast of South America, but each one was a dead end.

The Spanish captains grew more and more suspicious. Did Magellan really know where he was going? Or was he completely and utterly lost?

By now the fleet had been sailing for months and the seas were getting rougher and more dangerous. After surviving a terrible and dangerous storm, Magellan found a safe bay where they could spend the winter. He had read that, in the far north, the seas become gentler in summer. He thought that the same must be true in the south so decided to wait for better weather. The crew were put on <u>rations</u>, eating penguin and shellfish to survive.

Two of the Spanish captains still didn't believe Magellan. The stars in the sky didn't seem to match up with their maps. Rumors spread that Magellan had a secret plan to return to Portugal, taking all the Spanish goods with him. The day after arriving in the bay, the two captains decided to seize control and head back home to Spain.

As Magellan enjoyed an Easter meal aboard the *Trinidad*, two rowing boats silently paddled up to the *San Antonio*. Armed sailors boarded the ship and arrested all the Portuguese crew, murdering the ship's master. The *Concepción* and the *Victoria* were both seized in the same way, meaning three ships were now completely under Spanish control.

Magellan came up with a daring plan. A rowing boat was sent to the *Victoria* with a "message." While the Spanish captain was distracted, another band of Magellan's supporters boarded from behind and captured the ship. Magellan now had three ships, and the *San Antonio* and *Concepción* were trapped in the bay—with his cannons pointing right at them. There was no escape, and they had to surrender. Mutinying officers were usually executed on the spot, but Magellan forgave most of them.

He sent the *Santiago* to explore nearby coasts,
but it was shipwrecked. Its crew made the long
walk back to the bay to pass on the bad news.

Finally, the weather improved and the remaining
four ships headed south. Spanish officers again
asked him to turn back and to reach the East by
sailing east, but Magellan refused. He still believed
that somewhere the Atlantic would join up with the
ocean on the other side.

On 21 October 1520, the look-outs spotted a gap in the coast. The *San Antonio* and *Concepción* were sent ahead, while the other two ships waited and were battered by a fierce storm. Two days later the *San Antonio* and *Concepción* returned, firing their guns and cannons in excitement. They had found what looked like it might be a way through!

The whole fleet set off to explore and found a maze of bays and channels that never seemed to end. On they went, mapping each bay and dead end.

By 8 November, some of the Spanish officers on board the *San Antonio* had had enough. They waited until they were out of sight of the other ships and sailed back to Spain.

After 38 days of exploring the channels the remaining three ships finally emerged into a vast and wide sea.

It was so calm, and so beautiful, that Magellan named it Mar Pacifico, "the peaceful sea"—the Pacific Ocean.

Magellan had no idea how big this unexplored ocean was, or that crossing it would almost kill his entire crew. He only knew that the Spice Islands lay on the other side, and he was determined to get there.

First, the three ships sailed up the coast of Chile. After crossing the equator, they headed west. It was two months before they spotted any land. This turned out to be two desert islands, surrounded by waters infested with sharks that were too disgusting to eat. They had no choice but to carry on sailing.

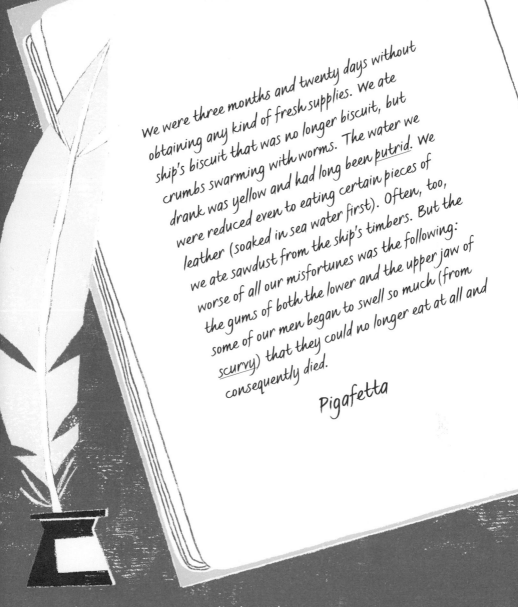

We were three months and twenty days without obtaining any kind of fresh supplies. We ate ship's biscuit that was no longer biscuit, but crumbs swarming with worms. The water we drank was yellow and had long been <u>putrid</u>. We were reduced even to eating certain pieces of leather (soaked in sea water first). Often, too, we ate sawdust from the ship's timbers. But the worse of all our misfortunes was the following: the gums of both the lower and the upper jaw of some of our men began to swell so much (from <u>scurvy</u>) that they could no longer eat at all and consequently died.

Pigafetta

In total, twenty-one men died on the voyage across the Pacific.

On 6 March 1521, the three ships finally reached an island where they could drop anchor, at Guam in the Mariana Islands. Here, they ate fresh food for the first time in 99 days, but they also attacked the local people to punish them for trying to steal from their ships. Pigafetta was horrified by the violence of the crew.

With full bellies, and helped by strong, steady winds, the fleet covered the next 1,500 miles in just ten days. They landed on a small island in the Philippines, where they found fresh water and caught wild pigs to eat. A few days later, they were greeted by people from a local island. Magellan swapped gifts with the islanders—red caps, mirrors, combs, and bells in exchange for fish, <u>plantains</u>, bananas, and coconuts.

Magellan began a friendly relationship with the islanders. They learned some of each other's languages and Magellan showed them the precious spices he'd come to look for: cloves, cinnamon, pepper, and nutmeg. The islanders told Magellan that the Spice Islands were indeed nearby.

After eight days, and plenty of coconut milk, the crew were recovering from scurvy and ready to sail again. Magellan continued exploring the vast archipelago. To his delight, they soon came across natives who spoke a similar language to his slave Enrique. They must be getting close!

But then Magellan got distracted. He became good friends with the king of Cebu, an island at the edge of the Philippines. After persuading the king, and many other locals, to <u>convert</u> to his own religion of Christianity, Magellan decided to try and convert other islands too. This was a huge mistake ...

The rival chief of the nearby island, Mactan, refused to obey the king of Cebu and change his religion. Magellan was feeling over-confident by now and decided to teach him a lesson.

In the middle of the night, Magellan took 60 men to attack Mactan.

Had it not been for our poor captain, not a single one of us would have been saved in the boats, for the others were able to withdraw to them while he was still fighting.

Pigafetta

When they waded ashore, they found 1,500 inhabitants waiting for them, armed with poisoned arrows and bamboo spears. Magellan and his men were knee deep in water and were attacked from every side. Magellan fought for more than an hour, before he was wounded by a poisoned arrow and, finally, killed by a spear.

With Magellan dead, there were not enough crew or captains left to pilot three ships. After burning the *Concepción* so that no one else could use it, Pigafetta and the survivors set sail for the Spice Islands.

With the help of local pilots, the *Trinidad* and *Victoria* finally reached their destination in November 1921, over two years after setting off from Spain. Every cannon was fired in celebration.

The mountainous islands lived up to the crew's dreams: local markets were bursting with cloves, ginger, rice, coconuts, plantains, almonds, pomegranates, sugar canes, cocoa, melons, cucumbers, pumpkins, and guava.

The final challenge was transporting these treasures—and news of their new route—back to Spain. The *Trinidad* was rotting and leaking too badly to make the voyage back, so it was left to be repaired. Some of the crew were so terrified at the prospect of another long trip, they decided to stay in the Far East, too.

The *Victoria* was packed with precious spices and set off for Spain, commanded by the Spanish sailor Juan Sebastián del Cano.

It was a daunting task—not only would he have to sail along the routes controlled by his Portuguese rivals, but a lone ship packed with treasures was a likely target for pirates.

This time, luck was with them. The *Victoria* reached Spain in September 1522, but with only 18 of the crew that had set off three years earlier. They had sailed more than 80,000 km and proved Magellan right: it is possible to set off in one direction and keep going until you return to where you started. They had completed the first voyage to circumnavigate the world!

The first
circumnavigation
of the globe

Enrique survived the battle of Mactan. He didn't trust the Spanish captains to free him, as Magellan had promised in his will, so he escaped. No one knows where Enrique traveled next.

The orange line shows the route that Magellan took

The green line shows the route that del Cano took.

Although he died in the Philippines, Ferdinand Magellan became famous as the driving force behind the first voyage around the world. Pigafetta's diary showed that it was Magellan's fearlessness and stubbornness that kept the expedition going.

Magellan's voyage led to these important discoveries:

There was a way past the huge continents of the Americas. The Strait of Magellan became an important route.

Strong winds around the equator helped ships to cross the Pacific more quickly. These became known as "trade winds."

Earth was MUCH bigger than anyone had realized and it really is a sphere.

If you travel around the world from east to west, you live through an extra day compared to someone who has stayed put.

Today, it is not only a strait that bears his name. The Magellan space probe to Venus, the Magellan Telescopes in Chile, and the two galaxies known as the Magellanic Clouds have all been named in honor of one of the greatest explorers the world has ever seen.

TIMELINE

1480
Ferdinand Magellan is born in northern Portugal.

1490
Magellan gets a job working as a page in the queen's court.

1494
On June 7, Spain and Portugal sign an agreement called the Treaty of Tordesillas, to divide newly discovered land between the two countries.

1517
Magellan moves to Spain and begins work on his new plan: to prove it's possible to reach the East by sailing west. The king of Spain agrees to fund the expedition.

1519
On September 20, the fleet set sail from Spain. There are five ships and more than 230 men.

1520
Two Spanish captains grow suspicious of Magellan and decide to seize control and head home to Spain, but Magellan comes up with a plan that forces the mutinying crews to surrender.

1521
Magellan makes enemies in the Philippines. He is shot with a poisoned arrow, then killed with a spear on April 27.

1521
Magellan's ships continue without him and in November they reach their destination, over two years after setting off.

1522
On September 6, the last remaining ship returns home to Spain, almost three years after the expedition began.

1496

Magellan is promoted to the rank of squire and works in the king's marine department.

1505

Magellan joins a sailing expedition to India and the Far East. The expedition lasts almost eight years and Magellan fights in several battles.

1513

Having returned to Lisbon, Magellan volunteers for a dangerous mission to Morocco and begins planning his own voyage to find a new route to the Spice Islands. The Portuguese king does not support him.

1520

One ship is shipwrecked and one ship abandons the voyage. In October, they finally find a route that links the Atlantic and Pacific Oceans.

1521

On March 6, Magellan's ships reach the Pacific island of Guam.

1521

On March 16, they reach the Philippines.

Today

2019 is the fifth centenary of the start of the first voyage around the globe. Magellan is celebrated around the world and remembered for his determination and courage as an explorer.

Ferdinand Magellan

GLOSSARY

archipelago—a group of islands.

cannibal—a person who eats the flesh or organs of other humans.

channel—a long, narrow body of water that joins two larger bodies of water.

circumnavigate—to sail or travel all the way around something, especially the world.

continent—one of the world's seven major areas of land. The continents are Europe, Asia, Africa, North and South America, Australia, and Antarctica.

conver—to persuade someone to change their religious beliefs.

doldrums—parts of the Atlantic Ocean and the Pacific Ocean around the equator where the winds are often calm and light, meaning ships can get stuck there for days or weeks.

equator—the imaginary circle around the earth that is halfway between the North and South Poles.

estuary—the wide part of a river where it meets the sea. Here, fresh and salt water mix.

expansion—increasing something in size, volume, or quantity.

expedition—a journey taken for a reason.

Far East—a geographical term that refers to East Asia.

govern—to rule or lead.

javelin—a spear thrown as a weapon in battle or hunting, or a long pole thrown for distance in an athletics field.

lance—a weapon with a long pole and a pointed head.

marine—relating to the sea or shipping.

mutiny—open disobeying or fighting against the leaders in charge.

page—a young person who worked as a servant for a person such as a king or queen.

pike—the tip of a spear.

plantain—a fruit that looks similar to a banana, but is less sweet and firmer. Found in tropical climates.

putrid—decayed and having an unpleasant smell.

ration—a limited amount of something that one person is allowed to have, especially when there is not much of it available.

rebellion—organized opposition against something or someone, often the people in charge.

scholar—a person who has studied a particular subject for a long time and is an expert.

scurvy—an illness that is caused by not having enough vitamin C in your diet.

squire—normally a teenage boy who has been a <u>page</u> and has reached a certain point in his training. He can now train to be a knight.

slave—a person who is wrongly bought by another person and is forced to work for them without pay.

INDEX

CREDITS

Photograph on page 61 courtesy of
the Library of Congress